Dorothy Baird

Mind the Gap

Indigo Dreams Publishing

First Edition: Mind the Gap
First published in Great Britain in 2015 by:
Indigo Dreams Publishing
24, Forest Houses
Cookworthy Moor
Halwill
Beaworthy
Devon
EX21 5UU

www.indigodreams.co.uk

ISBN 978-1-909357-85-3

British Library Cataloguing in Publication Data. A CIP record for this book can be obtained from the British Library.

Designed and typeset in Palatino Linotype by Indigo Dreams.
Cover design by Ronnie Goodyer at Indigo Dreams
Printed and bound in Great Britain by 4edge Ltd.
www.4edge.co.uk

Papers used by Indigo Dreams are recyclable products made from wood grown in sustainable forests following the guidance of the Forest Stewardship Council.

For Kirsty

because no poems about her
made it through the editing process
into this book

Acknowledgements

Acknowledgements are due to the editors of the following publications in which some of these poems first appeared: *Acumen, Artemis, Cinammon Press, New Writing Scotland, The North, Obsessed with Pipework, The Interpreter's House.* Some poems were highly commended in the following competitions: *Second Light, Ware Poetry Competition, Poetry Kit Summer Competition, and Poetry Space.* The poem *It Never Stops* was featured on BBC Radio 4 in Ruth Padel's programme on writing workshops.

Thanks are also due to Helena Nelson of Happenstance Press for her insightful comments on some of these poems

Other publications by Dorothy Baird

Leaving the Nest, 2007, Two Ravens Press

CONTENTS

Mind the Gap

The Poetwoman

after Pie Corbett

The poetwoman carries her poems
in the pocket of her pinny.

She stirs one in the pot of soup,
slips one in between the cheese
of her children's sandwiches,
hangs one out to dry beside the socks.

She stitches poems in the bones of leaves
so they open in the hedgerows in the spring

slides one in the purse of the tired woman
at the checkout, scatters them
like daisies in the park, folds them
in the biscuits in the old people's home,
tucks one under a swan's wide wing.

When the sun sets, she shakes her pinny
over the cat's dark fur, so any unfinished
poems fall into its warmth. When the cat
pads out into the night, her lines
brush against bushes and walls, attach themselves
like burrs to be read by moonlight.

Search

Swifts zip and dart
   looking desperately
for something they're sure
 was here
        no there   no over
   there by the tree   the fence
     the roof

      Soon
     they'll start to think they've
left it
     thousands of miles away
near a shimmering beach
 or a dusty tree
    and
     will set off
dipping and swooping
  till they get there

    where something'll make them
 wonder if
     perhaps they were
right first time
        so they'll leave
  the hazy plains
  and fly
    the thousands of miles
back here

to search all over again
still hoping to find it
under the eaves of the barn
over the fields
    or the telephone wires
here
            no
                    there
    no

Easter

The garden understands Easter
better than I do. It does not
pause to question stones
rolling from caves:
it only holds its breath through chill mornings
when haar blurs the sun, knowing
how winds blow into the heart of trees
and whisper blossom, how branches

sense the steady rise of sap, how tulips
cup their secrets in clasped hands
ready to redeem them in warm air,
how the huge wheel
creaks against the flow of days
shifting us towards
the only proof we need.

Hands

Let me stand breathing
before the sycamore tree
that knows in its own breath
the intimation of spring

and sends out two small hands
folded together in a pink capsule
that falls away when I touch it,
and then two more hands after that

and two more still, each pair opening
to let light leech
the blood rust of their birth
and green flow in.

Poetwoman explores the nature of time

1
She stirs the past
watches stories surface

remember when
remember when

those moments where a choice
or chance decision
meant she veered towards
the point that's now, leaving
untold possibilities
floating in the mix.

If only if only

She stirs the future too, but that's so huge
she stops. There's only so much uncertainty
she can cope with
and her arm grows tired.

2
She's seen on TV
how the starlight
we believe in
is the last signs
of its dying. So

it's puzzling out there,
where time is a word
unutterable

in the silence

of so much space

where perhaps there is
a parallel poetrywoman
in her rain-stained shed
contemplating stars and stories,
living in the only place she can,
where pigeons coo in the sycamore tree
and a squirrel skitters off the roof.

Miss Littlewood's Gift

In a world of twinsets and pearls
she was an outcast
in her man's shirt and tie
her bunched and belted trousers.

While others sheltered
behind their desks, she leapt
among us haranguing, cajoling,
wheedling us to pay attention

and when our lethargy
drove her mad, she'd clutch her hair
as if she could pull from its roots
another way of reaching us,

for it was her mission
to stoke in us a passion
for the power of language
the savage beauty of a line

but more than that: she strove
to wake us up, to shock us
into the risky business
of being ourselves.

To my son who wanted to be a bird

To become a blackbird
first you must rise daily at dawn
and learn how morning enters your bones.

Then you need to study the significance
of gold, the history of black,
and write a treatise on why this bird
wears shadows on its wings
and sunrise on its beak.

When you notice your heart dances
at the flick of a worm,
you are nearly there. If you spy
the slink and pad of cat
with a flutter of distress,
you come closer still

and when you stand on the rusted swing
and sing as if the whole world was song;
when time becomes the wind
ruffling the nape of your neck
and you long to stretch your arms
into its lift and fly
                        – then, my dear,
you will be more bird than boy
and my loss
will be the morning's gain.

Only so much me I can handle

Days are when I'd
rather be a blues singer
in a bar in New Orleans.

Or a mapmaker
calibrating contours
in the gas-fired warmth.

Or even a roofer
perched like a bird
on the gable end

wrapped and gloved
against the cold, resisting
the lure of the van.

Point of View

Can cats think? This one
looks like it can. Its pink nose
twitches. 'You're writing
rubbish,' it says

in cat language. 'Why sit
at this table, still as a tree
when there's lovely big darkness
through the flap

with its rustlings and scrabblings,
its cooling paving stones,
and its black grass
to pee on? You're

a funny thing,' it purrs
as it positions itself on my paper
and breathes its faint stink of mouse
or bird or both.

On the Verge

Where land crawls down to sea
and slips beneath waves
is a half and half place: a verge
where footprints vanish like a sad man's smile
and dunlins and sanderlings scuttle
before rising like smoke into the more definite air,
where shells sink in the scratchy embrace
of their broken selves, and the ocean
keeps its secrets to itself.

Into this almost space where sky pinkens
in that transition time of gloaming, they walk,
the two of them: she with the globe of her almost child
floating in its not-quite sea, he with his eyes on the horizon
where the sun sinks below the line
that isn't there.

They are not quite parents, not yet
landed out of the swell, where her hands rest
as if divining the future that's curled up
on the cusp of arriving.

Plate Spinners

dashing   through the forest of poles
      tweaking   circling   so they
keep spinning,   eyes on stalks
    for the wobble   that'll tip
the axis   the fall we might
 just   stop

  and rushing
     crazed dervishes
         from one to the next
     till all
we can see   is
    one teetering plate
        after another
but we keep   running   keep
    spinning
      to save the world
  from small
       shatterings

The Balance Sheet

Blue tits swoop across the lawn
from cherry tree and rowan
to the black hole of the box
tacked to the wall of the shed.

All afternoon I watch them
with their missile accuracy
target the circle that holds
those mouths that call
and call and call
as no punch sheet ever can
to keep them on the job.

I'm in awe of such parenting.

Though soon they'll get their cards
as those cramped wings
follow the urge for light
and the young mouths become silent
in the task of living.

Whereas here in this house
it's been over twenty years
and still the job rolls on.

Names

So hot, it is the summer
that never was. Windows
in my small shed
are wide with air, the weir
is loud. On my desk

a plum stone and a pen.
Today I face the afternoon
open as the window.
A bird sings but I
do not know its name.

A dog barks. It is nameless
too. Sometimes I call
my children the wrong name.
They mind as I would.
How much is gathered

there for us in sounds,
how much they give us
ourselves. The bird
finds itself in song. The dog
barks itself against

the rush of water and we
who say oak and elm
geranium plum daughter
bring a new edge to the shape
of their flowering.

Devotion

Witches abroad tonight
with their hats from Tesco
and their faces blenched like illness.

Plastic pumpkins swing from hairy fists,
rattling with malteasers, lollipops, the loot
of pound coins, monkey-nuts no one
wants and a few blowsy satsumas.

               Behind them
in the shadows of hedges, lurk
mothers, fathers, following like acolytes
these craven offspring, recognized
only by their shoes.

Hallowe'en

When you were wee, we hung doughnuts
from the pulley, dooked for apples
with a fork dropped in a basin. You
watched every move as I cut
a slanted smile, triangled eyes
in the pumpkin
so it grinned at tea.

Tonight you smear treacle on a scone,
swear as it swings against your mouth,
plunge headlong and sticky to drown
a stalkless apple, dunk your wet face
in an upturned bowl of flour to tongue
the slipping sweetie. The pumpkin you
carve is a punk, its scars glow
when it's lit. Later, you stomp
to your room, cackling.

                    When you emerge,
your eyes are red, face white, throat slit
with blood.

When you were little, you had nightmares
about the troll on the bridge, wept
at the lonely duckling. Off guising
tonight, your cloak swirls down the hall,
darkness spits on your shoulders
like a cat.

Thirteen on the Thirteenth*

A golden birthday, so they say,
and it's true: the sun gilds you
in your pink hat and spikey hair

as you glow around the house
singing, 'Come What May' at the top of your voice
gliding to your teenage years

as if they are a dress you've coveted for weeks
and now, finally, slip into its delicious folds,
you, who have been practising for months

the querulous eyebrow, the despairing
roll of eyes, that thud of the door
slammed on the old fools.

* Becoming the same age as the date is seen by some as a special birthday.

Typical

She claims, that in amongst
the undergrowth of papers, files,
discarded clean and dirty clothes,
furring tumblers, an odd spoon,

CDs, letters, old belts, terminally divorced
socks, she knows exactly
where everything is. I have to believe her,
when, in a challenge at noon, I demand

her ticket to the Scotland/Ireland rugby
game in 2009, the torch her granny gave her
two summers ago, the T shirt she tie-dyed
at Guides in January – and she, without pausing

in her mumbled song (her ears grow wires)
excavates, and, with a few flicks of her wrist
and a long-suffering drumroll of eyes,
deftly unearths each one.

The Exchange

He arrived today. Didn't speak.
Smiled. He has a nice smile.
He ate my food. Went to bed.
Didn't leave his sponge-bag
in the bathroom.
His dreams will be in German.
His thoughts will be in German.
He will tell his mother
about our house. Will he tell her
it is tidy? It is so tidy
the rest of us are on edge.

His blue eyes, fair hair surprise
me in the kitchen where
he stands awkward in socks,
language slipping away from him.

I smile too, rummage in a dusty brain
for words I can give him
like a gift he can hold – I see
he's holding on
to everything that's made him
who he is, here in our house
where he must create himself
with every syllable
of this halting tongue.

Bridge

Pull your skirt down
is my morning mantra;

I'm wearing leggings
is her 17 year old reply

(as if a vast expanse of thigh
is mitigated by
slightly thicker black).

Text if you're going to be late,
is my evening refrain;

the click of a departing door
is all her answer.

Oh build me a bridge across
the thirty years between us

with staunch pillars to withstand storms
and cables to support us.

Build me a way we can walk
over to each other's country

or even stand on the half-way rise
breathing in the blue of the sea

together.

It Never Stops

The antennae that once woke me
to catch a hiccup
before it revved to screams
now scan the quality of night
to read who's out, who's in.

And 'out' means stravaiging
in pubs and clubs, daundering
on streets with chittery bumps
they don't feel, lurching for
taxis, friends' floors, the last bus,

while I'm the missions' sergeant
in my wakeful nightie,
alert for keys, creaking
stairs, the sloosh of taps,
counting them home.

First Year

Yesterday we drove him to uni.
Tipped all his stuff
on to the floor of a tiny room.
I'll sort it out he says, though
he never did at home.

In the kitchen they stand
backed against the units,
their faces mirroring his
bemused expression
at being dropped out of family
into this flat where the only rules
will be their own.

He shoes us out.

I hug him, catching
my breath again
at the size of him
and leave,
quickly.

On the way home, you're content
to be in the empty car
looking forward to a cup of tea.

I think of him
discussing cupboard space
learning names.

Mind the Gap

We've survived her rucksack packing –
the forced discarding of dresses, shorts
and tops. We've survived

the photocopying of passport and insurance forms,
the writing down of addresses for postcards
she'll forget to send and the reassurance
of a name she'll never call but I'm glad to know

she could. We've survived the M8 in rush hour –
eight lanes going nowhere with the clock ticking
and the airport hovering like Emerald City.

We've said goodbye to her bag with its hopeful label for Oz,
gone up the escalators and been relieved
(though neither of us says it) to have to wait
for her last burger and chips on Scottish soil

for what seems eternity. And we've
reached the point where the next step is
Departures, Security and Go To Your Gate
and I don't know if I push her or

she pulls away, but she disappears,
small daughter with my heart
stowed in the pocket
of her very short shorts.

After She's Gone

We're dazed by a silence
in which we hear not Paulo Nutini
belting it out and bothering the neighbours,
but blackbirds and the dizzy hum of a bee.

In the uneasy quietness
we reclaim a space
where the washing basket is never full
and only two towels hang on the rail.

In strange corners I keep finding
(like sloughed off skins) a stray sock,
a pair of curled up tights,
the twisted wishbones of her kirbygrips.

Starting Over

More and more it's just the two of us
at the table that once sat five.

Ask before helping yourself
You need to eat at least some of the fish

are redundant phrases now
and the chat and teasing of our family meals
are tucked away with the booties and the vests.

Of course, he's not a stranger, this man
who is the children's father, but his face
is out of focus after all these years

and our words are tentative as if we're
in our twenties, sending out feelers:

Would you like to see a film?
What did you think of the book?
Look, it's started to rain.

Fruiting

In the warm earth
of your body
something is stirring
though it is not spring
but late summer.

It has taken root
with the fierceness of the determined,
and prepares to flourish in you
as the apple tree and the plum tree
flourish in your garden.

And I wonder
how this fruiting started
how it decided or how it simply happens
that this new growth buds, blooms
readies itself to fall

The Close of Day

A small spit of rain
to finish the day. Sun
that almost lasted
until dark. Now in the light
of an evening's silence
I sit, still as a stone
cooling.

Three hundred miles away you sit
too, because standing
is too tiring. Your body
betrays you with a flowering
that will one day leave
no room for breath. And

you will go, where stones
and rain and darkness
have no place. Where evening
is always, or morning; where
language breaks against
the absence of everything,
and our questions gather
like rain clouds
at the end of a summer's day.

Birthday Flowers

Today, you will wake up
if the drugs let you, and lie
against the pillows. It's

a celebration of the day
your dark hair crowned
your mother's warmth,

when you squalled at light,
air, noise, the touch
of everything. Now you face

another crowning. Out of light,
noise, air. To a place
hands can't reach.

We haven't learned
to speak the new language
this deserves. Instead we stumble

on the phone, send flowers in a basket,
a cradle of oranges and yellows,
the colours and scents of spring.

Saying the Unsayable

As the tumour ate her
more than she ate anything,
she still cooked stews for us,
simmered stock from bones,
pulled a pudding out the freezer.

We didn't mention her dwindling
but it hovered
in the silences at mealtimes
where she perched like a bird
picking at seed.

One afternoon, she gave the children money
for the shopping mall
while she took to her bed.

When her grandson returned
with a black shirt
in a bag from Next,
she shot a bolt of humour
dark as the shirt:

That'll come in useful!

and shuffled off
to make the tea.

Ceremony

A circle of ten on a Yorkshire moor
with a flask of ashes.

We scatter them on to heather and stones
passing the flask from hand to hand
as once we might have shared lemonade,
only this time no one's laughing.

Some drift in the wind
to find their own resting place.

I am surprised by how much there is,
but still am afraid that being last in the round
the flask will have emptied,
and I won't get to shake her
into the sharp moorland air, and then
feel ashamed for such pettiness.

Even in death, she is there for us all.

I lay the flowers on the ground: carnations
exotic against heather roots.

No one knows what to do next.

No one speaks, except the wind
howling in our ears. I wish I was
honest as that wind.

Slipping

In her garden raspberries are rotting,
brambles just turning from tight knots
into the soft baubles that, this year,
won't stain her hands.

She used to make bramble and apple pies,
plum chutney, summer pudding, but
those culinary fingers, like her green ones,
have not touched us, so we sit, shared out
round the table to avoid her
gap, with ready meals in front of us,

feeling she's hovering
over the crumby carpet, the tablecloth
that's seen better days, the plates
without napkins, badgering us
to go and pick her fruit
before the crows and blackbirds do.

Never Mind the Gap

In a box under her bed, we found letters
we'd written from hot countries

when we never considered the separation
mothers live with like a secret pain,

                          and a teddy,
wrapped in tissue paper and labelled:
For My First Great-Grandchild

like a portent of something
we hadn't even contemplated,

like she wanted to be involved
no matter how great the distance.

Wearing My Mother's Pearls

Even after a year, they smell of her,
as if hoarding in their moons
molecules of perfume, essence of her

transcribed into light and locked
in the blue velvet box, so that
when I finger the lustrous string,

she's here again, and something large
and almost tangible fills me:
is it loss,

            that sharp truth of never again?
Or a sense of connection
as if the scent materialises her

staunch spirit and straight spine, as if
she's approving me looking nice for once,
pearls warm against my neck,

their first touch of air since her fingers
stumbled with the clasp, undressing
after dinner in that last hotel.

'If you wanted to write about death, what words would you

- 42 -

choose?'

The Bard's intrigued. He strokes his left temple
as if treading in a holy place. 'I'd need,' he says,
'a new language to do it properly. I'd need
an entry into silence, a key
for the wrung out heart of grief.
A cracked mirror to pass through
into reflection. A breeze that is the last breath,
a cough, a rattle, a whiff of light
mutating into air. Why,' he pauses,
'what would you do?'
                    Poetwoman lifts her pen (a guitar
is playing in the midday sun). 'I'd choose skin
scented with summer, a woman relishing morning
under her downie, nasturtiums with beads of rain
sliding on their leaves, rosemary in olive oil,
the shining always-ness of water, the first wriggle
of toes in the sun, and – ' he's watching her now,
'let people read between the lines.'

Wondering about God

Of course she wonders: she's alive, isn't she?
And science hasn't yet explained the spark
that even in a test-tube
ignites a fledgling consciousness

and she's heard the forest's full of pine-cones
each shaped to the same mathematical formula

but TV plunders her with pictures of space –
its million million suns – and reason
is a task master for disbelief.

So she swithers. Some days she's a skelf of a shell
sucked out by a random, infinite sea.
Others, she's stopped by an autumn leaf
its precision, its beauty, its place.

Arriving

When I crawl out the car
after forty miles of single track roads,
switch-backed and stunning,
every bend a more outrageous view

that I daren't stop and savour,
being driven to arrive – I skitter
like a crab, suffering a raw softness
in its exposure, its risky search for home.

Retreat

She has come to Ardnamurchan
to the end of the western mainland
where the single track road stops

as if even it, with all its tarmacked bends
snaking across moorland,
recognises the superiority of sea.

She is looking for poems in the immediacy of wind,
the hurl of rain against caravan walls,
the hope of sun flaring through cloud.

She knows they are probably everywhere
– in the white sand, the ruined crofts,
in basalt and granite, thistles and rowans,

but first she has to empty herself
of the blindness of the city; still
the deafening turbulence of her thoughts,

so she can stop like the road
and see if she can translate, honestly,
their elemental language into hers.

Kilchoan Time

You can tell enough of time from the direction of the ferry
chugging like a toy across the water
one way or the other. This

is what a holiday does: throws clocks
out the window. Turns you again
to the way light wakes and dusk settles,

to the way nothing much matters
except how wind, rain and sudden sun
sculpt you back into yourself.

She hasn't spoken to anyone for a week

The wind has blown through her
and the gulls shrieked around her
and the sea, the lovely loquacious sea,
has said as much as it wants
and not expected a reply.

So it's been easy to be all ears
and simply listening.

Could this last for ever, she wonders,
or would she, in the end,
be found gossiping with the sheep,
arguing back at gulls?

A Question

I'm learning how rocks burst from hollow chambers
in spouts of fire, how they've shifted and settled
through century after century, while battles
have been fought and lands cleared and families
come and gone, while purple loose-strife,
foxgloves, ragwort, brambles, thistles, nettles,
rowan trees and birch have flowered and fruited
in the salt air
           in which I find myself now
watching the sea pulse over the stones
asking what does my life mean?

Believers

They approach quietly, like sheep
sidling up to a hedge before rain.
One radiates compassion
for me, who's twice her age,
and ready perhaps, being alone,
to be welcomed into the fold.
They proffer a magazine
from a quilted shoulder bag.

Oh my dears, what brings you here,
to this hamlet of one shop and a diesel pump,
where the sea and sky offer all the light
any lost soul could need, where
a congregation of clouds sings
each day in the westerly wind,
where truth is in every step
over the juniper and sand?

Without Witness

On my own in a caravan
overlooking the Sound of Mull
rain thrumming on its old roof

I think of you at home, dozing as you do
on the couch (daughter on lap-top
or out tip-tapping on too high heels)

but after five days amongst the hills
my thoughts float over the Sound
like the tuwhit of a seeking owl

but there's no tuwho because there's no you
to reply and now I'm not even sure
you exist or if you're memory's

quirky trick because you're fading
and, knowing nobody here, I can walk
into the shop and be anybody

so which of my possible selves
will I pull on today: one with husband and daughter
or the one untrammelled as the tides?

The hills are strewn with juniper and bog-cotton
and, frankly, do not care. After twenty-five years,
you are my long-haul witness, carrying the truth of me.

But you are far away if you're anywhere at all,
and I'm in a rain-drummed box,
eyes full of wind and sea.

Encounter

Something in my day-pack clinks
as I swing out over the miles
through the gloom of the pines.

He appears through the trees
and stops on the narrow track
for me to pass. I smell his sweat.

Bit steep, isn't it? I say because silence
is impossible. *Gets worse* he says
and laughs and moves away.

Friday 26th July 2013

I write the date as if its precision
might fix this moment, here
in a tent in Arisaig –

where I hear wind
bellowing in the pine trees, flapping
the rigging of ropes, the sails

of the door – but why?
When nothing around me
is still: not the clouds roiling

across the sky, not the grass
whipping like crazy on dunes, not
the waves pummelling sand, not

the children, tossed and tipsied
by cold water and shrieking
like gulls, not my heart, out

of the wind in the tent
of my body, beating
Let go, Let go?

Either Here or There

There is a way of walking by the reservoir
when there is only the water's wing-beats
against the shore and the hills
in their shifting colours, the wrinkled light
of mud furrowed by bike tracks and the wind
through the railings, moaning
like ghost-breath over bottle tops.

And there's another way when the path
just carries you – and the hills and the water
dissolve into conversations you wish you
hadn't had and thoughts about deadlines
and bills and the leaky roof, and suddenly
you're back at the car
an hour older.

Useful Gods

Beside me on the table Buddha sits,
his hands portioning the air
in the shape of acceptance that somehow

fits the angular cows, the slow
passing of the Ganges in the sun,
but here in Edinburgh

where peace and equanimity
hide in fractured time, he is a memory
of travels, not a god to wish upon,

and if I choose, the 'O' of the sellotape,
next to him, is just as potent a reminder
of life's eternal round.

New Year

We're penitents – bowed heads,
hoods, a slow walk
into the wind that offers
no absolution but tears at our jackets
and whips sand in our eyes

so we cling to each other
and wonder at dogs' innocent joy
as they streak from waves to the dunes
dropping a salted shoe
or a piece of wet wood at our feet.

We're here for the exercise
but resolutions are wavering
and the word *Café?*
half lost against the sea's roar
is seditious music to my ear.

Dear Mother, this is snow

The sky has torn itself
into whirling scraps
or it's a goose
shaking its feathers,
or fragments of amnesia
remembered and spilling back
into space – I don't know,
they call it snow
and snow goes white
and blurring, snow goes
smudging lines and rubbing
out the football pitch,
people's hats, the cars,
all white and soft, and feet print
new words on these strange pages.
It's water on my tongue, and
in my hand, so cold –
did I mention it's cold, mother?
It's a taste of metal, a shiver,
a hand-packed snow-stone
arcing through a swan feathery sky
to splodge
on a jacket or a tree, its hush
a shoosh,
a stillness like a baby sleeping.

Barra Ferry

Nodding off in the sun
next thing I'm up at the rails with the rest of them
gasping for the shock of their *Ooh!*
and a splash that's not the wake.

It rises again and I see it,
black, white, huge: a torpedo
up to the light, it loops and arcs
glistening back into the sea
with a farewell of a tail
that tells of whale. *Oh!*
we all go, *Oh! Oh! Ooh!*

Horgabost

A gale force wind
wrestles all night with our tent,
tugging guy ropes and pegs,
whipping its poles, snapping
the flap of nylon, as if
determined to wrest it
from the grass and blast it ,
over the white sands
towards Beinn Dhubh
like a belle-dressed ghost
or a Hebridean angel
jangling Celtic death songs
in the ropes of its lyre.

The Shape of the South

Poetwoman wears her thermals from October
to May (and sometimes, camping, in July).
Her whole life is bound to the central heating,
her hot-water bottle, woollen socks.

She wonders about her thyroid, walks for an hour
to get warm. Shivers at her computer
because her old house is draughty and it's too expensive
to put the heating on for one.

One summer, the sun shines. Outside,
writing, she sheds clothes piece by
piece, her feet released from thick wool
to the fresh air – she feels hot. Yes,
hot. And the fragrance of warm skin!

       Her words are tempted
    to go skinny-dipping
in the loch and
          plunging
    into peat pools!

Ah... she retreats to the cool of the cottage
puzzling over all that would change
if she lived elsewhere and heat poured
every day
from the scorch of a southern sky...

The Tale of the Internet

I've been sitting for hours,
the little hand waving me on
like Hansel and Gretel following the robin
deeper into the forest. And like the children,
with their shiny pebbles in the moonlight,
I could – if I wanted – retrace my steps
back through the forking paths
to where I started. I keep going.

Day is fading as it does
even when I'm paying no attention.
But here at my desk, the indefatigable screen
is all brightness and intrigue.

Top 20 remote places to visit before you die?
Five secrets you must know about cheese?
See what the baby chimp did, left on its own –
the cutest thing ever?

Oh yes, click
yes, click
yes

Breaking Up

He's in the yard
fixing his bike
growing hot
at rusted brakes
mudguards that don't fit
the intransigence of darkness
that hustles in too soon.

The child is pond-dipping
on the computer,
clicking bugs
and dragonflies
in the fake rustles
of a summer forest.

She sits at her desk
wondering how
it all fits together
how the years that hold them
hold them so lightly.

Some bugs will always rise
to the surface, some summers
always end
before you're ready,
some things
just can't be fixed.

Talking to each other can be hard

It's the meaning that misses its mark:
the gesture of intent
that fails somehow
in the space between lips
and the other's ears

as if the water of words
becomes muddied by air,

or the other's listening heart
has its filter on askew.

Veteran

They called him a hero
but put him on a waiting list for a house.

They called him a hero
but sacked him when his temper blew.

They called him a hero
but when he felt the night fracture

and the park in town become a desert
leaping with IEDs it was four months
for an appointment to get help.

He thinks he is the only hero
for whom a seashore of gannets
is too much killing

and starlings murmurating in the cold sky
mirror smoke billowing
after a bomb.

Messages

Listen, the dead are talking.
Can't you hear them in the wind
blowing from the east?

In the sound you can't place
of two stones knocking together
under the hedge? Can't you hear them

in the skirl of sea against the rocks,
in the drone of traffic pushing
up the A9? Can't you hear them

going on and on about all the stuff
that's staring us in the face?
They've squeezed through again

but just like before, no-one's listening
even though they howl through the trees
making the rooks flap and wheel.

Waiting Room

She comes out of the X-Ray
hand hidden in a bandaged stump
blood streaked down both arms
skittish with shock.

She tells me of wineglasses and stretching
and slipping and customers' faces
at the pools on the floor. *Such a bright colour,*
someone had said. *At least you're healthy.*

So we wait, as Sunday evening ticks by,
with the swollen eyes and limps and awkwardly
held elbows. Kids, with their injured mum, call out
'Hiya' to two policemen whose uniform is sober
among the blue scrubs and orderlies' green.

And we wait, learning about triage and wondering
about Hali Fillaza, who's somehow disappeared,
and watching chairs empty then fill again
as new cuts and sprains shuffle in.

She's updating her status with her left hand
and I'm thinking of all the things I'd thought
I would do this evening.

No one speaks to anyone else.

So when a man we've sat beside for three hours
notices us leaving and says, *All the best hen,*
we both stop, silenced,
before remembering to say thanks.

Poetwoman's Prescription

These poems are made of certified ingredients.
They have no contraindications, though
anyone with allergies (suspected or proven)
to metaphor, allusion, alliteration,
should take care.

Read them a minimum of three times a day
before or after meals. Do not read
whilst eating due to the high risk of
concentration loss and/or gravy stains.

If you miss one, read two at once.
You cannot read too many.

It is possible that a shiver of pleasure
is noticed, along with a rise in emotion.
This may increase when they are read aloud
and is no cause for alarm.

If the condition continues or deepens,
write your own poems and seek further advice.

In extreme situations, where help cannot be obtained,
urgently do as the Greeks did –
write the poem on paper,
and swallow it whole with water.

Turning Fifty

It's a new freedom,
with children venturing on their own path.
It's a new worry,
with children venturing on their own path.

It's parents,
who fill the time left by children
venturing on their own path.

It's padded bits around my hips,
and ambivalence over whether to
struggle or make peace with them.

It's envy (gently) at the young ones
with their peach-plum skin, and it's the awareness
I wouldn't want to start
all over again.

It's admiring white-haired women on the bus
with their lipstick and jaunty scarves,
and wariness of their thinning skin
as they white-knuckle the exit.

It's knowing growing old is the *best* option:
that death has no criteria for choosing
and it might come sooner,
not the later I live by.

It's blood drying up in a stop-start
severing of the contract
with the moon. It's hot flushes
and damp sheets: the fire and water
of a new baptism into Crone.

It's women friends,
who carry my scars as I carry theirs,
who recognise the medals
I won't be given.

It's my husband
who's woken up beside me
more than half the mornings I've been alive.

It's the blaze of fifty candles,
and the delight at still having the puff
to blow them all out.

School Lesson

I did the minimum of science: two years
of iron filings and blue overalls,
caustic smells and test-tubes held
with tongs over a Bunsen flame.

We never made it to the table
of elements, or the stars, just
cut up onion skins and hearts
of some dead animal we shrieked over
and Sheila had to go and see the nurse.

So now I'm in the dark, still, about the sun,
the tilting earth and tidal moons,
how plants grow and rocks are fired;
I don't know about gravity or pulleys,
the steam engine, blood circuits or

the chemical composition of gold,
and all the Latin and French in the world
won't help me understand the theory
of relativity or how infinity works.

But I can look at you and find
the words rising to my lips
of a poem by Lamartine
I was made to learn by heart.

Startling

It could be the last day I'll wake up
is a thought, barrelling in – from where? –
that catches my breath, like a forerunner
of the final gasp I'm afraid will be mine
sometime this fine day, where already

I've wasted two hours lying in. I begin
flinging on my clothes – the ones
sprawled like empty skins on the back
of the chair, then stop. Surely, today
of all days, I should take more care?

So I try pink against blue, patterns
against plain, each skirt or shirt
nudging me with its story. But half an hour

goes by, and I need to think about breakfast:
eggs scrambled, with pepper, a leaf or two
of parsley, chopped. The eggs
fall into the pan like the centre of gold flowers.
In their brown plastic pot, the frill of the leaves
thrills.
                              Goodness,
how extraordinary the day already is.

Edinburgh Fringe

There are some things I wouldn't do for money.
One of them is stand upside down with my head

in a bucket in the middle of Princes Street
(or indeed anywhere else). Even painting myself silver

from ear-lobes to toenails and standing still as the statue
I'm pretending to be, on a plinth in the Royal Mile

would be preferable. Although it must be hard
not to smile, not even a twitch of the lips

when tourists snap on their tablets or phones
then set about making you laugh.

Perhaps you have to send your thoughts into battle
(or wherever it was you heroically died), elevate above

the patrician crowds.. But at least
from the corners of your unblinking eyes

you can watch the tour guides fluster with their signs
or catch the steamy tango outside St Giles.

Unlike the man on his head in the bucket
waving his legs in the air like a tic.

Another Sort of Love Song

After all these years I owe you some words
so have these ones that find shape
hesitantly – it's not simple *to say*
even after all these years –

sometimes
   when you're asleep
I lay my hand against your curled spine
and, for a moment, imagine
empty space instead

and know then a grief
that says it all.

Indigo Dreams Publishing Ltd
24, Forest Houses
Cookworthy Moor
Halwill
Beaworthy
Devon
EX21 5UU
www.indigodreams.co.uk